THE SIOUX

by Robert Nicholson

Editorial Consultant: Ben Burt,
Museum of Mankind, British Museum

Scholastic Canada Ltd
123 Newkirk Road, Richmond Hill, Ontario, Canada

Copyright © Two-Can Publishing Ltd., 1992
Text copyright © Robert Nicholson, 1992
Edited by Claire Watts
Design by Fionna Robson
Story by Claire Watts

First published in Great Britain in 1992 by
Two-Can Publishing Ltd
346 Old Street
London EC1V 9NQ

Published in Canada in 1993 by
Scholastic Canada Ltd.
123 Newkirk Road
Richmond Hill, Ontario
Canada L4C 3G5.

Printed and bound in Hong Kong

Canadian Cataloguing in Publication Data
Nicholson Robert
The Sioux

Includes index.
ISBN 0-590-74360-0

1. Dakota Indians - Juvenile literature.
I. Title.

E99.DIN53   1993   j970.004'975   C91-095758-4

Scholastic Canada Ltd. would like to thank Cliff Summers for his counsel in the preparation of this edition.

Photographic credits:
By courtesy of the Trustees of the British Museum: p. 11; Bruce Coleman Ltd: pp. 6-7, p. 9 (top); Werner
Forman Archives: p. 9 (bottom left), p. 9 (bottom right), p. 16, p. 19, p. 22 (bottom left),p. 23, p. 30
(left), p. 30 (top right); Fotomas Index: p. 30 (bottom right); Peter Newark's Pictures: p. 13, p. 22
(bottom right)

Illustration credits:
Maxine Hamil: cover pp. 25-29; Zoë Hancox: pp. 3-24

Contents

All words which appear in **bold** can be found in the glossary.

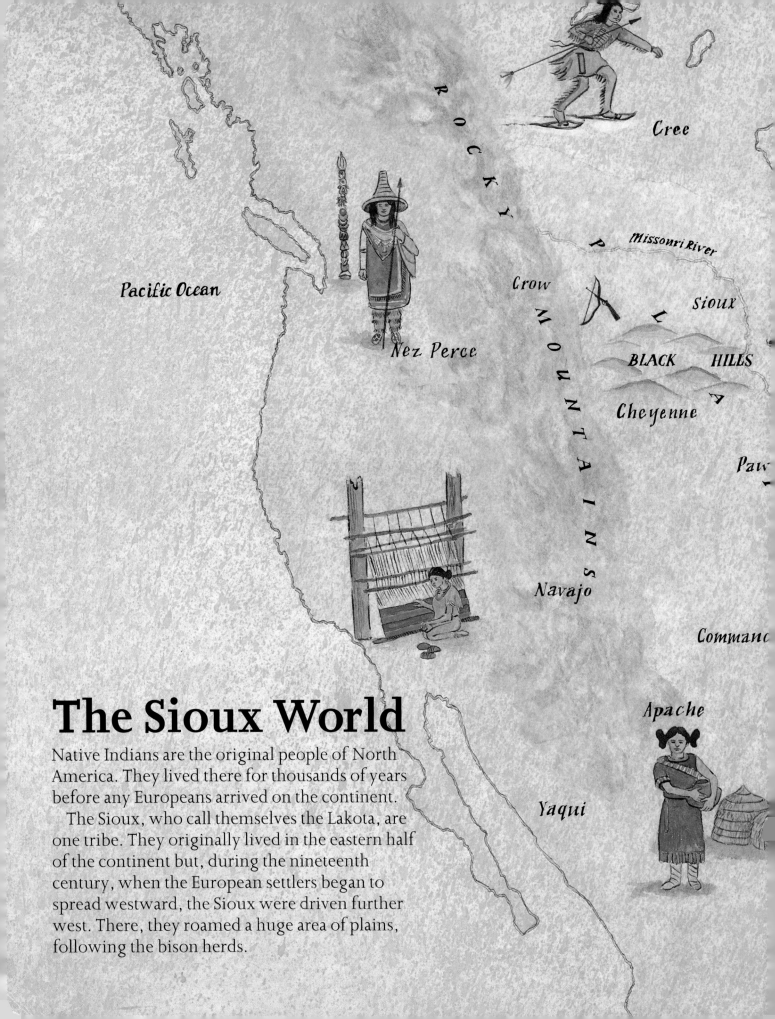

Cree

R O C K Y

Missouri River

Crow

Sioux

BLACK HILLS

Cheyenne

Pacific Ocean

Nez Perce

P L A

M O U N T A I N S

Paw

Navajo

Command

Apache

The Sioux World

Native Indians are the original people of North America. They lived there for thousands of years before any Europeans arrived on the continent.

The Sioux, who call themselves the Lakota, are one tribe. They originally lived in the eastern half of the continent but, during the nineteenth century, when the European settlers began to spread westward, the Sioux were driven further west. There, they roamed a huge area of plains, following the bison herds.

Yaqui

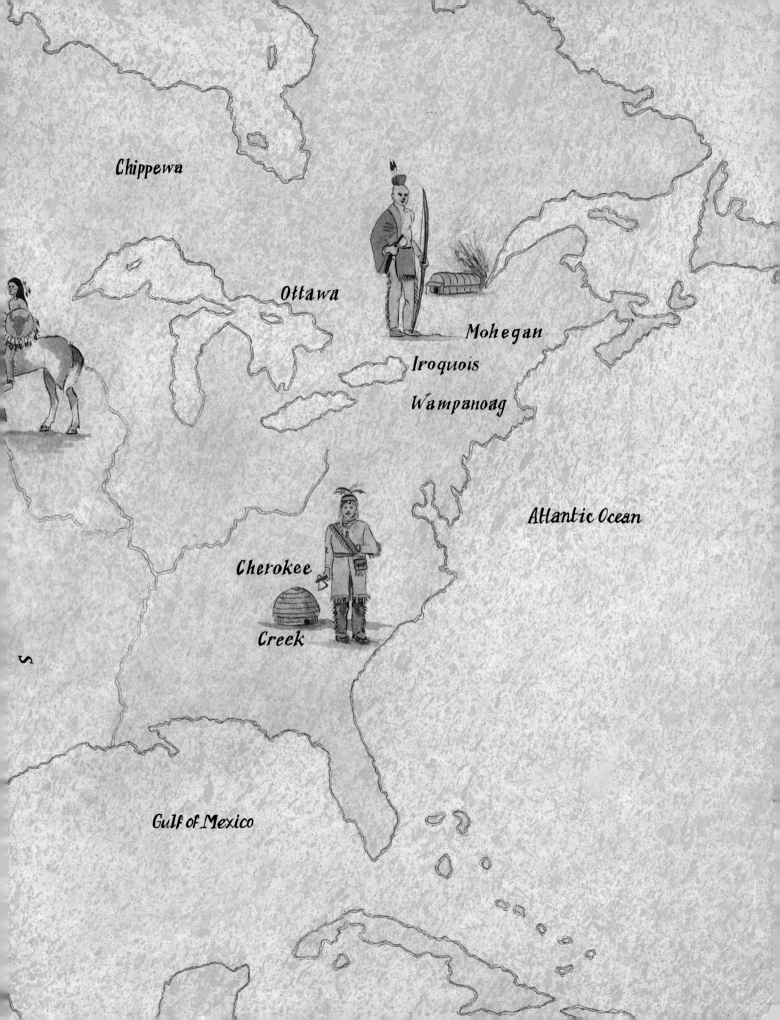

Chippewa

Ottawa

Mohegan

Iroquois

Wampanoag

Atlantic Ocean

Cherokee

Creek

S

Gulf of Mexico

Sioux Lands

The Great Plains area was very important to the Sioux. It gave them everything they needed to live – food, shelter and water from its rivers. The Great Plains also provided plenty of space and freedom for the Sioux to move about and to hunt and live as they pleased. Together with bison, many other animals shared the plains too, such as coyotes, wolves, hares and foxes. Antelopes, deer and bears lived on the plains and up in the hills.

The Sioux valued the land highly and realized how much they depended on it for their nomadic way of life. They believed that, when they moved camp, it was important to leave the places where they had been just as they had found them.

Bison and Horses

The bison was the most important of the animals that the Sioux hunted. Millions of bison roamed the plains, providing a constant supply of food and other materials.

The bison skin was a very important material, but a lot of hard work was needed to prepare it for use. First, the skin was stretched tight on stakes. Scrapers were used to remove any flesh and hair left on the skin, leaving the hide smooth. The hide was then rubbed with a mixture of liver, fat and brains to keep it soft and pliable, and then rinsed in a stream. Finally, it was softened by being pulled back and forth through a wooden loop.

▲ The North American bison has long, shaggy black hair covering its head and shorter brown hair over the rest of its body.

▼ Heavy loads were carried on special sleds called **travois**. Before horses were introduced, the Sioux used small travois pulled by dogs or people. Horses could pull larger loads much more quickly.

Shunka Wakan

The Sioux called their horses **shunka wakan**, which means sacred dogs. Before the Spanish settlers brought horses to North America in the seventeenth century, the Sioux only had dogs. Horses could carry much bigger loads than dogs and were much faster, enabling people to follow the bison herds over much greater distances. They also made hunting bison much easier and more exciting because hunters could chase the bison and shoot them from horseback. Horses were highly prized, and often the only way for a tribe to get them was to raid another tribe's camp.

Horn, Hide and Meat

The Sioux made use of every scrap of the bison.
● Horn was used to make spoons.
● Bones could be carved into knives or scraping tools to clean hides.
● A bladder made a good food bag.

● Skins or hides were sewn together for tents, storage bags and clothing.
● A skull was often painted and used in religious ceremonies.
● All the different parts of bison meat were eaten.

Bravery

There were many other native Indian groups on the plains besides the Sioux. To protect their rights to hunt and to prove their bravery, men of rival tribes fought one another. Warfare between certain groups, such as the Sioux and the Pawnee, could carry on for generations.

Warriors did not always try to kill each other. Instead they **counted coup.** They believed that getting close enough to an enemy to touch him with a hand or a coup stick was much braver than killing him from a distance with an arrow.

Brave warriors who won many honours also had many responsibilities. They were expected to protect the old and weak, and provide food for those who were not able to hunt for themselves.

Signals

All the tribes spoke different languages. They could communicate with one another using a system of hand signals.

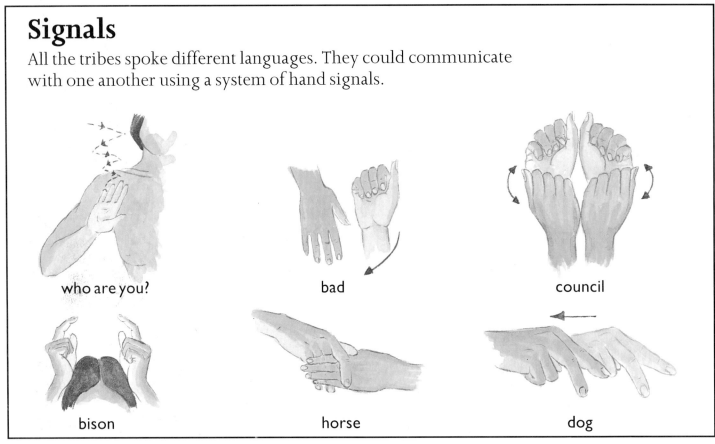

who are you? bad council

bison horse dog

▲ A coup stick, like this one, was decorated with feathers, beads and hair.

11

Famous Sioux

The Sioux who are remembered in history books became famous during the "Indian Wars" (see page 24). These leaders brought together rival tribes in the struggle to protect their lands.

▶ Many Sioux leaders tried to negotiate with the white soldiers, but with little success.

Crazy Horse

Crazy Horse was a Sioux leader who refused to leave the plains to the white man. When offered money for the Black Hills, or **Paha Sapa**, he said: "One does not sell the earth upon which the people walk."

Sitting Bull

Sitting Bull was chief of the Hunkpapa Sioux. He struggled for thirty years as a warrior and leader to preserve his people's lands.

Red Cloud

Red Cloud was chief of the Oglala Sioux. He kept the white man out of the sacred Black Hills for ten years, but was finally forced to accept life on a **reservation**.

Sioux Names

Sioux children were not given names when they were born. As they grew up, some young people earned their names by performing acts of bravery, and some were told their names by spirits in dreams. In the meantime they were known by nicknames.

The Tribe

The Sioux formed the biggest tribe of Indians on the plains, and were divided into several smaller bands. These are known by different names, such as the Hunkpapa Sioux and the Brûlé Sioux. Each band would split into small groups in winter, when food was scarce. In the summer, the groups from each band met at the summer **hoop**. There all the chiefs told each other what they had been doing, where they had hunted and who they had fought.

Each group was made up of several families that were related to one another. They had a chief who was the leader of the group. The chief could not force anyone to do anything they did not want to do. Above all, the Sioux regarded themselves as individuals, free to do as they pleased.

There were no laws among the Sioux. Instead a series of customs was taken as the guide to how people should behave.

Hunters and Scouts

Not all the men were warriors. In fact a few men did not fight at all. Some men were great hunters and knew all the tricks for hunting bison. Others were expert scouts and helped the band find bison or enemies. The man with the best memory was given the job of recording on a big bison skin what had happened to the tribe each year. Some men were camp comedians, and told jokes and wore funny clothes.

Women

Women gathered wood and wild vegetables and cooked food. They prepared bison hides for sewing, and made all the clothing. Although the men hunted the bison, it was the women's job to carve them up, making sure every bit was used and nothing was wasted.

It was perfectly acceptable for a man to have more than one wife, and often this helped to make the women's work easier.

Religion

Religion had a central place in Sioux life. The most important spirit was **Wakan Tanka**, the Great Spirit to whom the whole universe belonged. The people prayed to the spirits of their ancestors and those of the earth, the sky and the sun. The Sioux valued dreams and visions as a way of communicating with spirits and obtaining their protection. Each tribe had at least one **medicine man**, who could foresee the future, advise on spiritual matters and often heal wounds too.

Religious festivals took place at several times throughout the year. Men and women performed special dances and chants, usually to particular spirits. The **Sun Dance**, in summer, was the most important festival. Some men fasted for several days. They would pin their bodies with wooden stakes to a pole in the middle of the camp in the hot midday sun, hoping to have a vision. The Sioux believed that the men's courage would please the spirits and win their protection in the coming year.

▲ Each man had a pipe which he filled with bark or herbs. When a friend visited, the pipe would be lit and the men would smoke together. The smoke from different herbs was thought to be sacred.

Sweat Lodges

Water was poured on red-hot stones to make steam in **sweat lodges**. The heat and closeness purified and strengthened the spirits of the people inside.

The Lodge

Life in the **lodge**, or teepee, was ordered extremely well. Everyone had their own place to sit, work and sleep. It was bad manners to walk between the fire and other people - you had to move round behind them instead.

Building the lodge

● 25 bison skins sewn together formed the outside of the lodge.

● Long poles were lashed together with sinew.

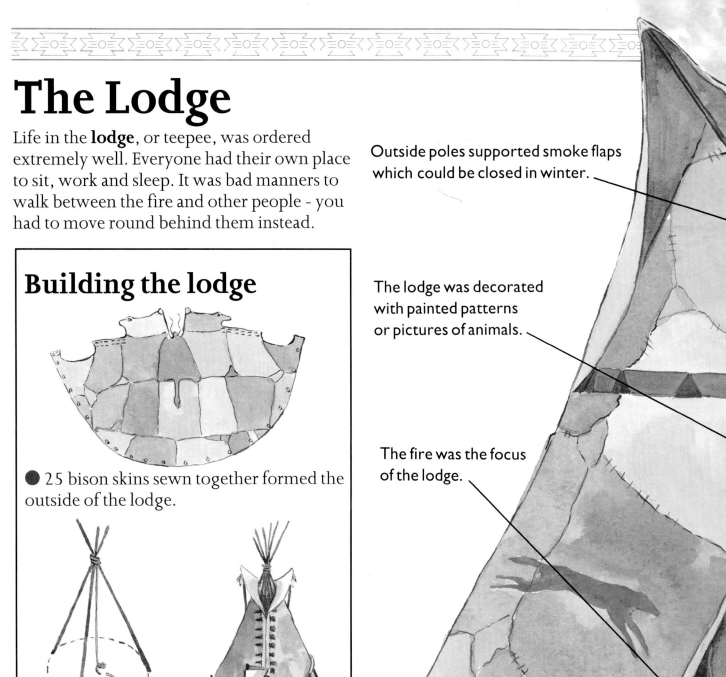

Outside poles supported smoke flaps which could be closed in winter.

The lodge was decorated with painted patterns or pictures of animals.

The fire was the focus of the lodge.

A back rest

Pots and cooking materials

Children

The Sioux thought that children were very important because they were the future of the tribe. They treated their children with great care and seldom punished them. The worst punishment was having cold water poured on you.

Boys and girls learned to ride when very young and by the age of six or seven were expert riders. By then, the girls would help the women with their chores, and the boys would be taught by the old men of the tribe how to herd horses. There was no school, so children learned about what they would have to do as adults by trying to do it.

Children had plenty of time for games. These would often be races, mock battles on horseback and other rough games. In winter, they made toboggans and went sledding.

▼ Children often made their own toys, but more elaborate toys, like this doll, would have been made by an adult.

▶ Babies were strapped to their mother's or grandmother's back on slings made from leather and wood.

The floor was covered with rugs made from hide.

Food

The Sioux did not grow their own crops or breed their own livestock, apart from their horses. Their food came almost entirely from the bison and wild plants which were all around them on the prairie.

Fresh bison meat was roasted or boiled. Cut into strips and smoked or dried, it could be kept to eat later. Dried meat was pounded and mixed with fat and berries to make **wasna** (or **pemmican**), a staple food especially good for travelling or in winter when fresh meat was scarce. Antelope and elk meat was also eaten.

Wild vegetables and fruit like turnips and berries were used to flavour meat, and made rich stew. Most Sioux women kept a pot of stew on the fire to offer to visitors.

▲ Before the European settlers brought metal pots, the Sioux used bison stomachs to cook stew. Hot stones from the fire were placed in the stew to heat it.

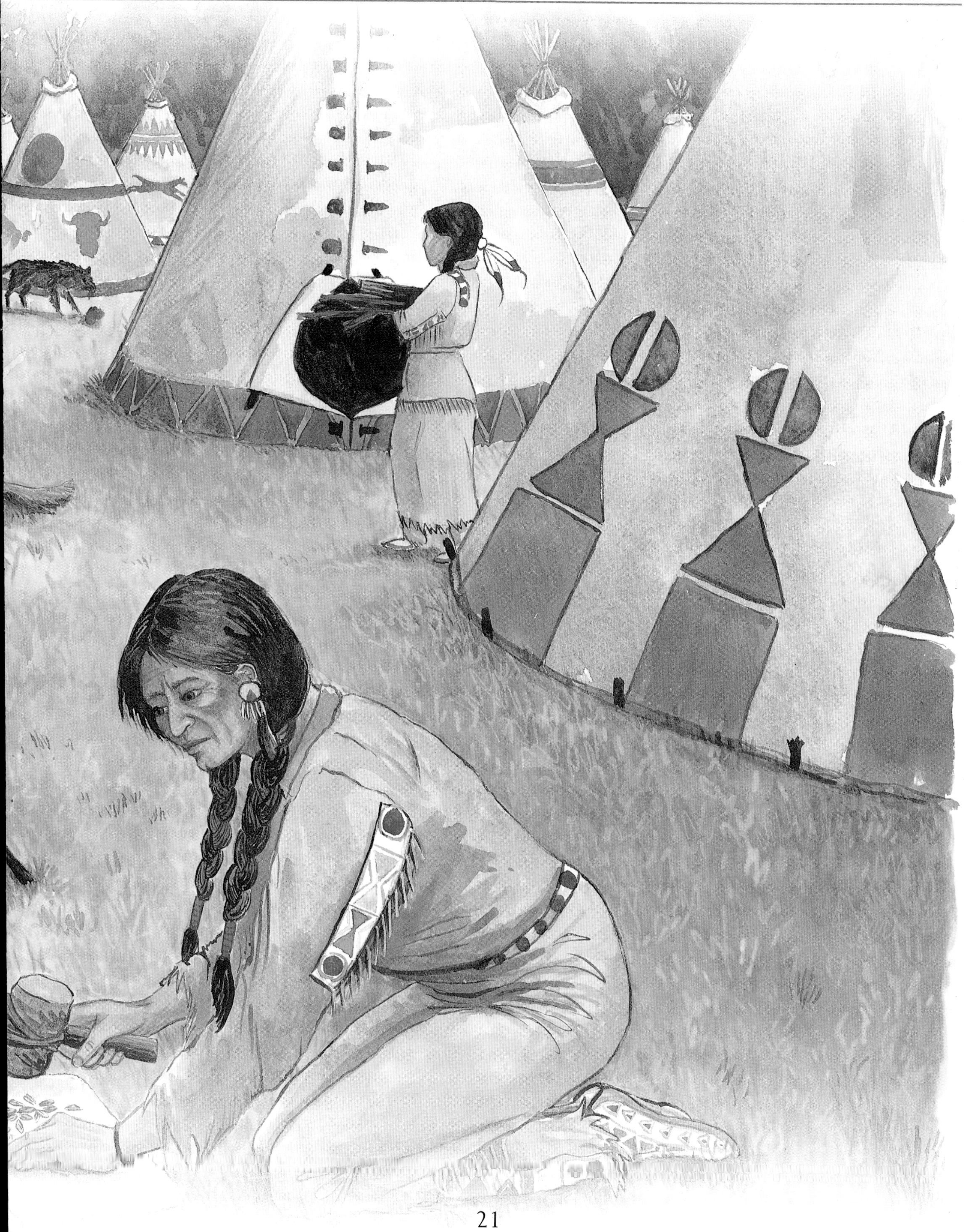

Clothes

The Sioux wore very simple, everyday clothes, but they had more elaborately decorated clothes to wear for special occasions, such as battles or ceremonies.

Men wore shirts and leggings, and women wore loose dresses. Everyone had full-length robes made out of a whole bison skin to wear on top. On their feet they wore **moccasins**, made from bison skin.

In winter, these clothes would be worn under warm thick bear skins, cloaks and full-length leggings.

On special occasions, successful warriors wore feathers in their headbands. Enemy **scalps** might be sewn on to a warrior's costume to show his achievements. Warriors and hunters painted their faces and the bodies of their horses with bright colours in striking designs which were thought to encourage the support of important spirits.

▲ Women would chew pieces of leather for a long time to make them soft enough to make into clothes like this dress.

Decoration

Sioux women were expert at decorating moccasins, clothes and **amulets**. They used paint or porcupine quills, which were hollow and so could be cut up and sewn on like beads. Moccasins decorated with beads were often made as a token of love for husbands, sons or brothers. Feathers were used to decorate lances, arrow quivers, shields, **war bonnets** and pipes.

▼ A Sioux warrior had to perform many brave deeds before he could wear a war bonnet. When it was not in use, the war bonnet was rolled up carefully and placed in a long bag to protect it.

Craft

Originally, the Sioux used dyed porcupine quills to make beads, but later they traded with Europeans for coloured beads. Try decorating some fabric with beadwork yourself. Work out your pattern first. Then sew the beads to the fabric one row at a time. Do not sew more than six beads with one stitch, or they will be too loose.

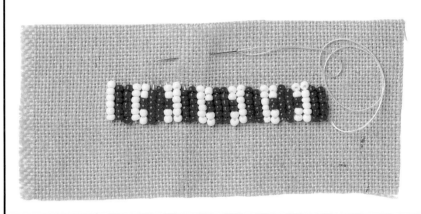

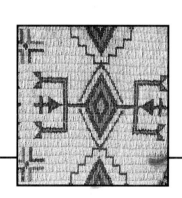

Feathers

Feathers were worn in the hair as symbols of honour. They might be cut in certain ways to record a warrior's acts in battle.

killed an enemy and took his scalp

third coup on enemy

cut an enemy's throat

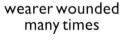

wearer wounded many times

killed an enemy

fourth coup

fifth coup

The Coming of the White Man

As more and more Europeans arrived in North America, they spread further west into the plains. They built railways, slaughtered bison, and fenced in land for farms, disrupting the Sioux way of life. The Sioux fought to defend their rights and their land. Although they won some battles, eventually the Sioux were overcome by the army. Native people of many tribes also died from diseases brought by the settlers and from starvation as the bison disappeared.

The Sioux and other tribes were confined to small reservations. Without room to wander, it was impossible to keep on with their traditional way of life. But the Sioux have not forgotten their traditions, and nowadays many Sioux people are returning to the stories, crafts, customs and religion of their ancestors.

Bison Slaughter

● In 1850 there were 20 million bison on the Great Plains.
● By 1889 only 551 animals could be found.
● Today, because they are now protected, there are about 15,000 bison.

The Crow Chief

The Sioux told many tales about spirits and about the world around them. This tale tries to explain why bison run from the Sioux hunters, even though the spirits were supposed to have created them to serve the Sioux.

The Sioux have always hunted bison on the Great Plains. Long ago, though, hunting was very different. The bison understood that the spirits had created them to help the Sioux to live, so they were happy to be hunted. In their turn, the Sioux treated the animals honourably. They never killed more bison than they needed, and they always asked forgiveness for killing a bison, and then gave thanks to the spirits.

However, the Sioux had one enemy: the crow chief. At that time, all crows had dazzling white feathers, and they were very wicked. Their chief did not like the Sioux, and so he told all the crows to perch on the broad backs of the bison and tell them not to let the Sioux hunt them. Whenever the crows spotted Sioux hunters approaching the bison herds, a cloud of white crows would swoop down, shrieking at the bison:

"Quick! Run for your lives! The hunters are after you!"

At this, the huge, dark herd would stampede away over the plain.

After some time, the Sioux could put up with this no longer. The Sioux chief called all the tribe together.

"We must catch the chief of the crows," he said. "The crow whose feathers sparkle like the snow is the leader."

"But how should we catch him?" asked a woman who sat near him.

"I do not know," said the chief, looking around at the gathered tribe "Someone must go alone amongst the bison."

One young warrior stepped forward. "I will go. I will catch the wily crow."

"You are brave," said the chief. "The medicine man will give you magic to help you."

So the young warrior went into the medicine man's lodge. The medicine man made a big fire with green, blue and pink flames. Then the medicine man dressed the young warrior in the heavy skin of a bison, and whispered magic words in his ear.

Outside the lodge, the tribe watched as smoke rose from the opening in the top. Suddenly, the tent flap was pushed to one side and a bison emerged. This was the young warrior, with the body of a bison, but the heart and the mind of a human.

The warrior made his way to the edge of the prairie. In the distance, he could see the dust rising as the bison herd approached. As they passed him, he joined the herd and ran with them. The bison did not know that they had a human among their number, because the young warrior looked and smelled like a bison.

27

On the ridges above the prairie, the hunters gathered, watching the herd. In the sky above the herd, a flock of white crows gathered, watching the herd and the hunters.

At a word from the leader, the flock of crows swooped low over the herd.

"Run for your lives," they screeched. "The hunters are after you!"

Bellowing with fear, the herd of bison stampeded. In a few moments, the prairie was empty, except for a cloud of dust and one lone bison, still munching at the grass.

The crow chief was surprised. No bison had ever stayed behind when the herd stampeded before. He swooped down towards the lone bison, screeching:

"Are you deaf? Run for your life!"

As the crow approached, the lone bison stood up on its hind legs and shrugged off the bison skin. Before the crow had realized what was happening, the young warrior grabbed its legs and tied them with a long rope. He tied a large stone onto the end of the rope so that the crow could not fly away.

Then he carried the crow back to the camp and took it straight to his chief. Outside the chief's lodge, the tribe was gathered round.

"You are a wicked bird!" the chief told the crow. "You have tried to break the sacred link between man and bison!"

With that he hurled crow, rope and stone into the fire.

As the tribe watched, the crow's brilliant white feathers were singed black as night. With a lick of fierce flame, the rope burned through and the crow soared up out of the fire, and flew away, cawing loudly.

From that day, all crows have been black as night to remind them to steer clear of bison and men.

As for the bison, they are more watchful than before. If a careless hunter makes too much noise, the herd does not wait to be killed. It disappears in a cloud of dust.

28

How We Know

Have you ever wondered how we know about the old Sioux way of life even though it came to an end long ago?

Evidence in Pictures

Each Sioux group had an artist who recorded the events of each year on a bison skin. Each winter he would paint a summary of what had happened that year. This was called the **winter count**. It is possible to date these records accurately from the information they give us. One winter count, for example, shows a bright light passing across the sky, which has been proved to be a meteor that was seen in 1822.

▲ This is part of a winter count done on cotton. Can you guess what any of the images represent?

▲ A few contemporary artists produced very accurate images of the Sioux. This picture by George Catlin shows two hunters creeping up on a bison herd.

The Popular Image

If a western film is on television, watch it carefully. Decide whether you think that it presents a true picture of native Indian lifestyle. How are the people presented? Does it show accurately what happened?

▶ Some Sioux artefacts show images of the struggle with the white man.

Evidence from Settlers

The North American histories and records show how the Sioux were seen by their enemies. However, few soldiers or politicians really understood the Sioux way of life. For example, Custer claimed that the Sioux treacherously broke the treaties that they had signed. But often these treaties were signed by only one group of native Indians, who could not represent any of the other groups. American records neglect to mention many of the times that the government broke treaties.

Glossary

amulet
a sacred object thought to give spirit power to the person who carries it.

counting coup
getting close to an enemy and touching him or standing facing him to show bravery.

hoop
summer camp when all the band came together. Lodges were arranged in a huge circle.

lodge
tent or teepee where a family lived.

medicine man
a wise man who saw visions and gave advice.

moccasins
soft leather shoes, often decorated with beadwork.

Paha Sapa
the Black Hills of Dakota which were considered sacred by the Sioux.

reservation
a special area set apart for native Indians to live in.

scalp
the hair of a defeated enemy, which was used to decorate a warrior's clothes.

shunka wakan
the Sioux word for horse. A rich man was a man who owned many horses.

Sun Dance
the biggest festival of the year, when sacrifices were made in honor of Wakan Tanka.

sweat lodge
small hide hut used in the sacred rituals.

travois
a sled made from two poles tied together with hide spread in between.

Wakan Tanka
the Great Spirit who made all things and allowed the Sioux to roam free on his land.

war bonnet
feathered headdress worn by great warriors to show their skill in battle.

wasna
dried meat with fat and berries.

winter count
a yearly pictorial record of the tribe's history.

Index